For Jon

This is Rosy Apples modelling
A beautiful vintage dress at
The retro festival, Newbury,
Summer 2015

This lovely country singer
Performed at Hemsby 2015
Rock and roll weekender

Busy applying make up at the
London Edge show in London
March 2015 !

Out at the Summer
of Vintage Festival
at Uttoxeter Racecourse
summer 2015

The very lovely Jayne Darling singing at the Summer of Vintage Festival 2015

Enjoying the sunshine at Tetbury
Vintage Fair May 2015

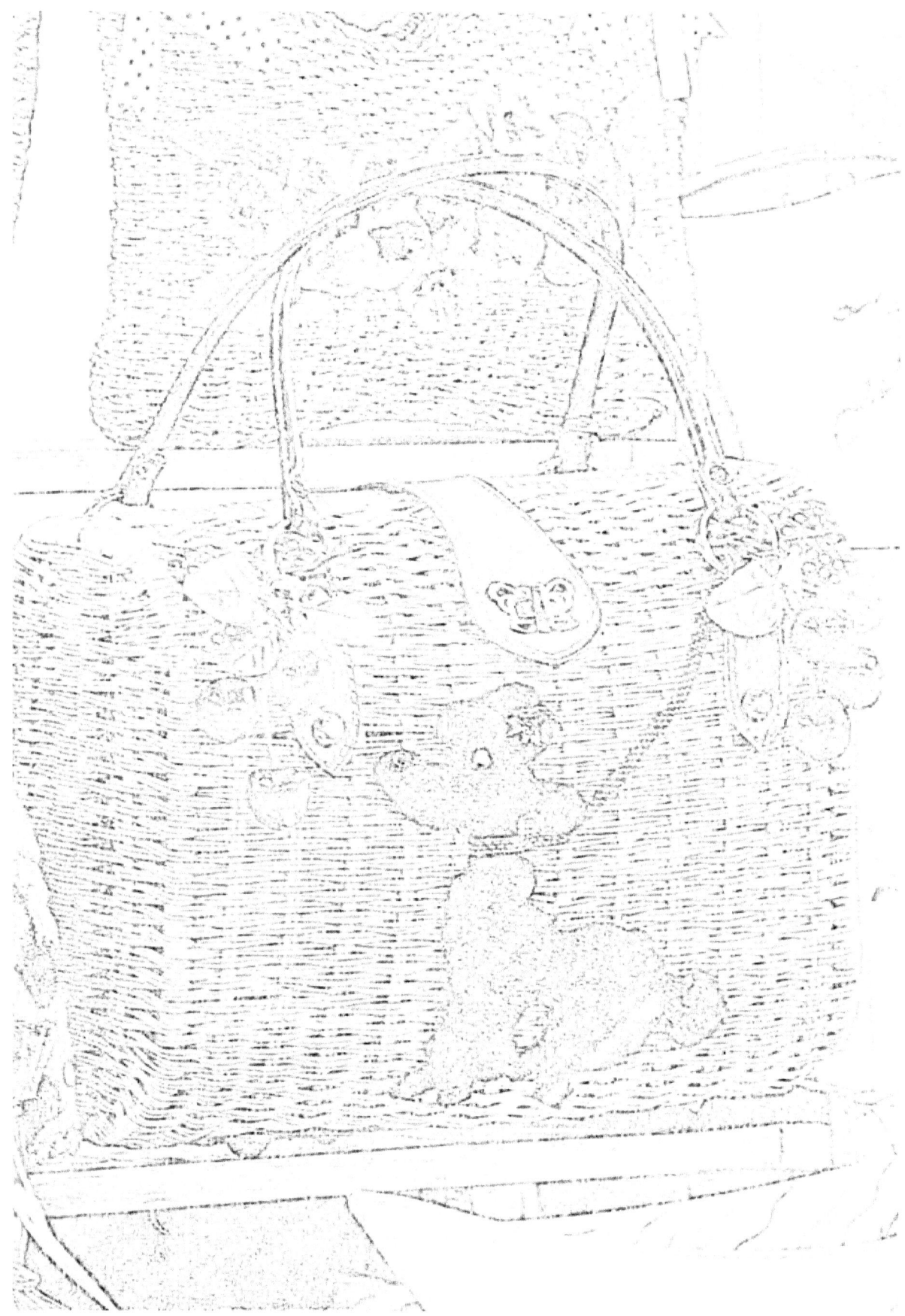

How we love retro
Basket handbags!
At the retro Festival,
Newbury summer 2015

The fabulous Bevin Boys Band at Milton Keynes Vintage Fair 2014

Dishin' up the teas
And food at the Retro
Festival, Summer 2014

Just hanging around at
Cherry Red Records
Stadium, Kingston, Surrey
September 2014

A thoughtful moment and
And a well earned break
At Summer of Vintage festival
2015

One very lovely and
Hopeful entrant in the
Fashion parade at the summer
Of vintage festival
Summer 2015

Shoes, shoes and more
Shoes! London Edge
Show Spring 2015

Hoping I will sell some
Vintage today! Leamington
Spa vintage fair 2014

A very wartime couple!
Summer of Vintage festival
Summer 2015

Is it the fabulous Baker Boys? At Twinwood Festival, August 2015

Enjoying the sun at the vintage
Festival, Morecambe, September
2015

Miss Tanya takes the floor at the Gloucester vintage fair 2015

Give us a twirl!
Retro festival
Summer 2015

Bexi Owen takes
The stage at
The vintage
Festival at
Uttoxeter 2014

Getting a hair cut at Yellow
Vintage Fair, Southampton
2015

Vintage curls and victory
Rollers at the retro
Festival, 2014

At the vintage fashion show, Retro Festival, 2015

Keeping a watchful eye at Twinwood
Festival 2015

Also from Michelle Hatcher:

The Vintage Eye guide
To 20th century Fashion

1940's Accessories handbook

Extraordinary Journey 2016:
A true story of Autism and courage.

Thank you very much for buying
This book.

www.ingramcontent.com/pod-product-compliance
Lightning Source LLC
Chambersburg PA
CBHW080325290526
45793CB00006B/1210